The Dating Game

Bible keys to winning at relationships

by
Dan Vis

All Scripture quotations are from the
King James Version of the Bible
Emphasis supplied unless otherwise indicated.

ISBN: 978-1-958155-09-7

Published by FAST Missions
111 2nd Street
Kathryn, ND 58049

Additional copies of this book are available by
visiting us at WWW.FAST.ST

Dedication

This book is dedicated to my grandchildren, who will soon be entering the dating game, along with a prayer that God will guide each one to just the right partner.

Table of Contents

The Dating Game
Preface

When I first became a Christian, I was just a young man, barely into my twenties. And I already had a long list of failed relationships under my belt. I didn't think too much about it at the time, as that seemed to be the normal order of things.

But God quickly brought me into contact with some dedicated Christians who suggested God might have a completely different plan for dating. One that didn't involve breakups and heartache. One that truly allowed God to lead in our choice of a life partner.

And I'm forever thankful, that I committed myself to that plan--as five years later, I ended up joining my life to the most wonderful companion a man could want.

But in all the years since, I can't think of a single sermon I've heard on the topic. That silence, in fact, has been deafening. And as a result, countless young people have entered into this phase of their life, unprepared and ill-equipped. Without even a basic knowledge of God's principles in this area, it's no surprise many end up in mismatched marriages, filled with regrets.

So for that reason, I've decided to jot down a few notes from those early years. It's been a long while since I've had to play the dating game, but God's principles are timeless and true. And they will work just as well in today's modern age.

If you are a young person today, I urge you to invite God in to the next few years of your life. It could very well lead to a lifetime of joy and happiness...

Dating and the Bible
Day 1

It's commonly said that the most important decision you will ever make is whether or not you will choose to follow Jesus—because that choice determines your ultimate destiny. And that your second most important decision will be who you choose to marry. That's because the person we pick for our life companion is going to influence every other decision we make from that point on.

A pretty solemn thought actually.

This suggests to me, at least, that the process by which we choose our life companion is important. Use the wrong methods, and you'll likely pick the wrong person. Use the right methods, and your odds of success go up. It's just that simple.

The term we use today to describe that process of choosing a partner is called dating. After all, other than in a few very rare cases, you are only going to marry someone you date first!

Dating and the Bible

It's been a long while since I've had to play the dating game, and things have certainly changed a lot since then. When I was a young man, there were no such things as dating apps like

Tinder and Match. And couples didn't communicate over Snapchat and Instagram. In fact, we didn't have cell phones at all!

But one thing has remained constant...

And that's the widespread assumption the Bible has nothing to say about dating. While it's true, you are probably not going to find that exact word in your Bible, that doesn't mean it has nothing to say on the subject. The Bible, in fact, is a fantastic textbook for building successful relationships. And it's full of relevant principles for choosing a life partner.

Think about it for a moment: if choosing a mate is indeed the second most momentous decision we can make—does it really make sense the Bible would be silent about it?

And take that one step further. If we are serious about wanting to help others climb higher in their walk with God, doesn't it make sense that we would want to understand those principles? And help teach those principles to others too?

Of course it does! And that's the reason for this course.

What to expect

In the days to come, I'm going to share a number of vital principles that together can help a person navigate this critical phase of life. Along the way, we'll answer a number of hot button questions, like:

How old should I be before I start dating?
What are dating's biggest do's and don'ts?
What if I'm lonely and don't have anybody?
How do I know if someone is right for me?
Is there any way to ensure lasting happiness?

I believe the answers to all these questions, and more, can be found in the pages of the Bible. And that its answers are reasonable, practical, and transformative. Follow them closely, and they will give you wonderful insights into truly successful relationships.

The Bible may not have much to say about how to spruce up your Tinder profile, or how to take better Instagram pics—but at the deepest and most fundamental levels, it will tell you just what you need to win at the dating game.

Dating and the Bible
Worksheet

What are the two most important decisions most people make in life?

1)

2)

What does that suggest about the importance of how we date?

What is one widespread assumption related to the Bible and dating? Explain why this assumption cannot be true?

Additional Notes:

Models for Mating
Day 2

In yesterday's reading, I mentioned that I have been out of the dating game for a very long time. I've been happily married to one woman my entire adult life, and I haven't the least bit of interest in looking anywhere else.

But that actually gives me a bit of an advantage when it come to understanding how the dating game works. Why? Because it gives me a bit of perspective. Through the years, I've seen a good many people get married, and have had the opportunity to see how those marriages worked out. In fact, I married a number of couples myself as a pastor—some of whom are going on nearly a decade of marriage themselves!

Watching things unfold like that over time gives you a different outlook. A young person in the throes of a romantic relationship often has a hard time looking past the emotions of the moment. But someone who has been watching marriages, and working with couples for decades, is well positioned to notice patterns. To analyze things from cause to effect.

Looking back over all those years, I've come to the conclusion there are just two main models for mating. And the model you choose has a huge impact on the success that comes after.

The Hollywood Model

The first model is what I sometimes think of as the Hollywood Model. I call it that because we see this pattern promoted endlessly in popular media. And unless we are exposed to something different in our own family upbringing, it's likely we've bought into this model to at least some extent.

It starts with physical attraction, noticing that cute boy or girl. After a bit of flirtatious behavior, a coupling takes place, usually the result of some expression of affection—like a kiss. Hollywood highlights this breakthrough moment, giving the impression they are now going to live happily ever after. But the reality usually looks far different.

More often than not, social pressure combined with youthful hormones cause the young man to press the girl for more romantic favors. The girl then consents, afraid he might leave if she refuses. The boy starts to lose respect for the girl, or begins to take her for granted. And then the girl, sensing this, starts to feel insecure, and asks for a more formal commitment. It's that "define the relationship" talk. The guy, feeling pressured, begins to back off, leaving the girl more frustrated and anxious. And more insistent. And before long, things have spiraled into arguments and various kinds of power plays by one side or the other to get what they want. Eventually, they break up, and the cycle starts all over again.

Not every relationship follows this pattern exactly—but enough follow these basic steps to suggest it is still pretty much standard operating procedure in most relationships. Just as it was in my day!

But I'd like to suggest this approach is deeply problematic. First, because it trains us to be serial daters. That is, we go from one relationship to another, sticking with each one only as long as the benefits outweigh the problems. Subconsciously, we internalize the principle—that when a relationship no longer works, we end it and move on to someone new. In essence, this model is training us for relationship failure. Every breakup is essentially practicing for divorce.

After enough failed dating relationships, we may eventually manage to weave our way through all those various obstacles and get someone to agree to marriage. But then the second problem comes in—all those past broken relationships. Each one damages some piece of our heart, leaving behind regrets, disappointments, and pain. And we bring these wounds into our new relationship—creating fresh fears, insecurities, and distrust. And all these issues complicate the marriage relationship. The more break-ups we experience, the more baggage we carry.

God, of course, never intended us to go through any of this kind of heartache, and it was never His will for relationships to fail. Which is why I believe the Bible suggests an entirely different model.

The Biblical Model

The biblical model reverses the order of things, moving physical affection from the front of the dating relationship to the end, and starts with a simple rule: keep your hands to yourself. It focuses on priorities like self-development and personal improvement. It involves building friendships with multiple people, as we interact with them at work and school and church. Social life revolves around group activities with others who share our beliefs, values, and interests. Essentially, this approach pursues opportunities to observe multiple potential partners, and consider each one objectively.

Naturally, some friendships will grow stronger over time. Often these will center on shared spiritual goals and ministry activities, with the goal being mutual growth—while avoiding the stresses and pressures of romantic, emotional attachments.

When it does become time to move that direction, it is done slowly, and carefully, and only after much counsel and prayer. They wait until God makes it clear to both parties that it's His will for them to explore a closer relationship together, and then they move purposefully and deliberately into an exclusive coupling, then engagement, and then marriage. The wedding, at last, is then a public testament to God's guidance in their life. And that marriage will be marked by a bedrock commitment to a lifelong union.

In an imperfect world, filled with imperfect people—things don't always work out this ideally. But I've seen it happen enough times in my life to believe anyone can have this experience. I am fully confident God can and will lead each one of us to the exact partner we need if we will but put His will first, and do our best to follow His plan for dating.

Or to put it differently, there's no reason a Christian should ever have to experience the heartache of a difficult break up. We can enjoy a rich social life while waiting for God to reveal His exact choice for our life partner. And then at the right time, we can enter into marriage with the full assurance God has led us into that union. The biblical model for mating leads to all these advantages and more.

The bottom line is clear: your model for mating has huge implications not only for who you end up marrying, but also the happiness you are likely to experience in marriage. Yes, God can heal and restore mismatched partnerships, but how much better to get things right from the start. Don't you think?

In the next couple readings we are going to look at essential biblical concepts that are key to pursuing God's plan for dating...

Models for Mating
Worksheet

Summarize in your own words what the Hollywood Model of dating looks like?

Summarize briefly what the Biblical Model of dating looks like

What are the advantages of God's plan over how the world typically does things?

Additional Notes:

The Ten Commandments
Day 3

I once heard an old pastor tell the story of a sticky situation he found himself in. He was visiting a family in his church which happened to have a teenage daughter. This girl was eager to start dating—but dad didn't think she was old enough. And he was determined not to let that happen.

During his visit, the young girl burst out with the question, "Pastor, how old do you have to be before you can start dating?" One quick glance at father and daughter, and he knew he was in trouble.

Here's the answer he gave: "You're old enough to start dating, when you are able to understand and commit to following biblical principles for dating." It was a great answer, actually—because readiness to date is not a matter of some fixed chronological age. It has more to do with personal maturity. Our spiritual development. Our commitment to God.

If those things are lacking, it doesn't matter how old you are—dating can lead to disaster. On the flip side, when we approach dating God's way, everyone can be enthusiastic about it. Including parents!

The Dating Commandments

Which leads to another sticky question. What are those dating guidelines? Or to put it differently, what is and isn't permitted for believers when dating? The Bible is pretty clear that sex before marriage, (also known as "fornication"), is expressly forbidden. See I Thessalonians 4:3, Ephesians 5:3, etc. But what about all those steps leading up to sex? Is holding hands ok? What about kissing? And so on, all around the baseball diamond.

In my pre-Christian years, I didn't worry about sexual attraction at all—the more the better as far as I was concerned. And I tended to get emotionally and physically attached right from the start. But once I became a believer, it became obvious this wasn't God's plan at all. And I found myself asking that same question about what was and wasn't permissible. So I set out to find some answers.

Basically, I started looking for verses that had clear principles related to dating. And then from these I built up a list of dating guidelines. These were rules I set for myself to try and ensure my relationships stayed within biblical bounds. I typed it up many years ago and still have a copy in my files.

Here's the list I came up with. Think of it as the dating ten commandments:

1) I will only date professed Christians.

Paul argued forcefully we should not be "unequally yoked together with unbelievers" (II Corinthians 6:14) because that makes it impossible to enjoy the spiritual intimacy God wants for couples. Mixed marriages were a chronic problem all through the Old Testament and it led to endless problems. And it still does today.

2) I will only date Christians who share my beliefs and values.

The New Testament repeatedly urges believers to strive for "the unity of the faith, and of the knowledge of the Son of God" (Ephesians 4:13). So it's not enough to marry a Christian—they need to be a member of your own denomination, with similar views and practices. Amos makes it clear that two people can't really "walk together, except they be agreed" (Amos 3:3).

3) I will only date Christians that are spiritual, and growing.

The Bible also makes it clear that not all Christians are spiritual or mature. Some in fact, are "carnal, even as unto babes in Christ" (I Corinthians 3:1). And that this leads to "envying, and strife, and divisions" (I Corinthians 3:3). So if you want true peace and joy in your home, avoid dating Christians who are weak in their faith.

4) I will only do that which I would recommend to a younger Christian.

Paul could encourage others to do "those things, which ye have ... heard, and seen in me" (Philippians 4:9), because he lived his life as an example to others. Even if something might be ok for us, Paul urged us to "take heed lest by any means this liberty of yours become a stumbling block to them that are weak" (I Corinthians 8:9). We should strive to live model lives.

5) I will not do anything I would not want done to my future mate.

We don't always know how a relationship is going to turn out, and it may be tonight's date will end up marrying someone else in the future. The golden rule applies here: do unto others as you would have them do unto you (Matthew 7:12). In other words, treat your date as you would want the person dating your future spouse right now, to treat them.

6) I will not do anything that would be inappropriate to do with my sister.

This may sound like an extreme principle, but it's the exact advice Paul gave to Timothy. As a young, single minister, Paul urged him to treat "the younger [women] as sisters, with all purity" (I Timothy 5:2). It's still good advice today.

7) I will not do anything that stirs up passion or lustful thoughts.

The Christian life is a constant battle between our spiritual and carnal natures. And we dare not give our flesh the least bit of advantage. "Be not deceived", Paul wrote, "God is not mocked: for whatsoever a man soweth, that shall he also reap. For he that soweth to his flesh shall of the flesh reap corruption" (Galatians 6:7-8).

8) I will not put myself in situations that lead to temptation.

If you are serious about wanting to win the war for dating purity, you are going to have to put some serious safeguards in place. "Make not provision for the flesh, to fulfil the lusts thereof" (Romans 13:14) Paul warned. And again, "let him that thinketh he standeth take heed lest he fall" (I Corinthians 10:12).

9) I will not engage in fornication, or those activities that lead to fornication.

Paul saw this as so dangerous, his advice wasn't just to resist sexual temptation—it was to run away, immediately! "Flee fornication" he wrote in one place (I Corinthians 6:18). And for that matter, "flee also youthful lusts" (II Timothy 2:22). If things start to get hot and heavy, it's probably wise to get out of that relationship as quick as you can.

10) I will avoid touching any woman in a sexual way.

Apparently, the church at Corinth was asking the same sorts of question about what was and wasn't appropriate in male/female relationships, and had written Paul for advice. His answer? "It is good for a man not to touch a woman" (I Corinthians 7:1). There's a place for human touch, but it's best to avoid that when dating!

Build Your Own

My advice is take some time and study this issue out for yourself. Find your own verses and write out your own dating guidelines. Or just start with this list and tweak it as needed.

Better still, get into some of the nitty gritty. Set a curfew for yourself—as our judgment gets fuzzy late at night. Limit the time you spend together, or on the phone—as the more hours you spend together, the more your feelings grow. Do group activities, or with each other's families and avoid time alone. Be proactive, and convert these basic biblical principles into a practical plan of action.

And if at all possible, do this BEFORE you get into a romantic relationship. Otherwise human nature is going to find some way to wiggle out of what these verses actually say. Our ability to rationalize poor choices is pretty impressive, actually.

And finally, stick to your rules. Commit to them prayerfully. Memorize your list of key verses. And periodically review your guidelines to keep them fresh in your mind. Your rules will only be as good as your follow through.

If you've already gone farther than is wise, you may need to sit down and have a conversation about it with God. And then another conversation with your partner, to try and recalibrate things. God is able to heal and restore relationships, but it always starts with a firm commitment to put His will first. If they are not open to growth in this area, that may be an indication it's time to terminate that relationship.

If all this seems a bit overwhelming, let me encourage you. In addition to giving us dating safeguards, the Bible also gives us a whole universe of dating possibilities. We'll be looking at those in tomorrow's study...

The Ten Commandments
Worksheet

What does this reading suggest is the right age to start dating?

Summarize briefly each of the ten dating commandments outlined in this lesson:

1.

2.

3.

4.

5.

6.

7.

8.

9.

10.

When is the best time to establish your own dating personal dating guidelines?

What steps should you take, if you have already violated one or more of these biblical principles?

Additional Notes:

Escaping the Black Hole
Day 4

Yesterday, we spent a lot of time looking at biblical guidelines that can help us discern what is and isn't appropriate when dating. Personally, however, I think the whole question is flawed from the start.

It's true that there are dangers when it comes to dating, and we need to put some firm guardrails in place to protect our self, and the person we're with. But looking at that list alone may lead a person to think: if that's all there is to dating, why date at all?

Well, the Bible actually gives us a lot of good reasons to date. Dating opens up all kinds of exciting and wonderful possibilities in life. And by learning to focus on those things the Bible calls us to pursue, rather than focusing on what it calls us to avoid—we can enjoy a rich and rewarding social life. And ultimately find that perfect life partner at last.

The Black Hole

Here's another way to think about it. Dating can be kind of like a black hole. There are all sorts of gravitational forces connected with it, working to draw you in, deeper and deeper. And the closer you get to that black hole, the stronger those forces become. Get too close, and you are going to be sucked in for sure.

But there is also a wide open dating universe all around you waiting to be explored. Rich, rewarding activities sure to bring joy to our heart. Given these two realities, is the question you really want to be asking how close you can get to the edge of that black hole without falling in?

That sounds to me like a recipe for disaster.

Dating Goals

I mentioned yesterday that I wrote up a list of dating guidelines, to protect me and anyone I was dating. But I also drew up a list of dating goals. These were positive things the Bible encouraged, that I could happily pursue in my dating relationships. And this list made all the difference in the world.

Here's another list for you to consider:

1) I will seek to glorify God by my dating.

Paul encourages us that "whatsoever ye do, do all to the glory of God" (I Corinthians 10:31). And that certainly applies to dating. Vi and I both had a strong desire to glorify God in our relationship, and while we didn't do everything perfectly, our dating experience is a true testament to God's power to bring two lives together.

2) I will seek spiritual growth in my dating relationships.

While Paul warns us to flee "youthful lust", in the same breath, he urges us to pursue "righteousness, faith, charity, peace" with those who are pure in heart (II Timothy 2:22). Investing time together in activities that encourage spiritual growth will prove a blessing to both of you, even if you don't end up getting married.

3) I will seek to learn to be a true friend.

Conventional wisdom suggests we do everything possible to stay out of the "friend zone", but the Bible encourages us to not only learn how to be "friendly", but to be "a friend that sticketh closer than a brother" (Proverbs 18:24). While in the process of settling on a life partner, I recommend trying to build healthy friendships with multiple people.

4) I will seek to manifest the true characteristics of love.

One thing I did early on was memorize I Corinthians 13:4-7, from Paul's great love chapter, and made an intentional effort to cultivate these various qualities. Dating relationships are an excellent opportunity to cultivate kindness and courtesy with our partner, and many other valuable character attributes.

5) I will seek to be open and honest in my dating relationships.

One of the warning signs of an unhealthy relationship, is secrecy—because that is usually an indication there is something to hide. But Jesus warned that "nothing is secret, that shall not be made manifest; neither any thing hid, that shall not be know and come abroad" (Luke 8:17). Strive to keep your relationship as open and transparent as you can.

6) I will seek to cultivate true self-control and integrity.

Paul tells us that it's not only God's will for us to "abstain from fornication", but also that "every one of you should know how to possess his vessel in sanctification and honour" (I Thessalonians 4:3-4). There's no better opportunity to develop these qualities than in a dating relationship.

7) I will seek to honor my parents (and my partners parents) in my dating.

All too often, there is conflict between parents and children when it comes to dating. But God promises that those who honor their father and mother will be blessed (Exodus 20:12). Striving to date in a way that respects both sets of parents will greatly add to the joy of that relationship.

8) I will seek to date in a way that enhances ministry effectiveness.

It's never too early to start thinking about our life work. In fact our first priority while "unmarried" should be caring "for the things that belong to the Lord" (I Corinthians 7:32). Marriage can greatly enhance our ministry, or it can leave us entangled "with the affairs of this life" (II Timothy 2:4). Doing ministry together is a great way to assess whether someone would make an excellent ministry partner.

This list is not exhaustive, and I'm sure you can think of other positive things to pursue in your dating relationships. But it makes the simple point that having clear positive goals in mind can help us shift our focus away from that black hole we need to avoid, and toward the wide open possibilities of learning and growing and interacting with people of the opposite gender. It makes these friendships positive, and worth pursuing.

Ultimately, in fact, this is what the whole Christian life is all about, isn't it? As Paul wrote to Timothy: "Now the end of the commandment is charity out of a pure heart, and of a good conscience, and of faith unfeigned" (I Timothy 1:5).

Or to put it differently, the whole point of the law is that we learn to love. That we learn to pursue every relationship with a pure heart. That everything we do should leave our conscience clear. And that it all needs to be driven by a sincere faith God will bless us in the end if we do.

That's biblical dating!

Escaping the Black Hole
Worksheet

Why is asking what we can and can't do on a date a flawed question? What is a better question?

List eight dating goals suggested in this lesson:

1.

2.

3.

4.

5.

6.

7.

8.

What does I Timothy 1:5 suggest the Christian life is all about?

Additional Notes:

The Gift of Singleness
Day 5

Want to know what I think is probably the single biggest secret to success in the dating game? It's our willingness to be single. Hear me out, as I explain what I mean...

Needy Hearts

Many people come from broken homes, and carry all sorts of baggage with them. I was certainly no exception. There were a lot of faulty family dynamics, and I grew up with a needy heart.

I started dating in my late teens, well before I had the maturity to know what I was doing. And once I got started, I went through a long string of unhealthy dating relationships—so many I can't even remember some of their names. I wasn't really thinking about what I could bring to the other person's life, but rather what I could get out of that relationship.

When I became a Christian at the young age of 20, I quickly made the kinds of commitments I've been sharing with you. And because I went to a small church, there weren't many real options for me. Zero, to be exact. So I went through a long period of several years without a single girlfriend. And I'll admit, it was a difficult, lonely time.

But God knew that was exactly what I needed. Because those years gave me time to build my relationship with God. To give the disciplines of discipleship time to work in my life. And gradually, my heart began to heal. When I was finally ready to focus more on serving another person, God brought Vi into my life.

Benefits of Singleness

Paul too, saw benefits in living a life of singleness, and strongly encouraged it. In I Corinthians 7, for example, Paul emphasize this more than once:

> *"For I would that all men were [single] even as I myself"* *(I Corinthians 7:7)*
> *"I say therefore to the unmarried and widows, It is good for them if they abide even as I" (I Corinthians 7:8).*
> *"As the Lord hath called every one, so let him walk" (I Corinthians 7:17,20,24).*
> *"This is good for the present distress ... it is good for a man so to be" (I Corinthians 7:26)*
> *"Art thou loosed from a wife? seek not a wife" (I Corinthians 7:27).*

While Paul makes it clear there is nothing wrong with joining our life to a partner in marriage (when the Lord so leads), he is clearly arguing that a single person is "happier if [they] so abide" (I Corinthians 7:40). In fact, that's the conclusion of the whole chapter: he that marries "doeth well", but he who marries not "doeth better" (I Corinthians 7:38). Paul goes so far as to say the ability to stay single is a gift from God (I Corinthians 7:7)!

Now while we may not see singleness as a gift, or feel called to a life of singleness—it's worth understanding the benefits Paul outlines in this chapter. That way, those who find themselves single, can know how to make the most of it.

From my study of this chapter, Paul gives at least three distinct benefits to being alone:

1) It allows us to focus more fully on God. I Corinthians 7:32-34
An unmarried person can focus entirely on "how he may please the Lord", but a married person has to divert at least some focus to "the things that are of the world, how he may please his wife". A single person can focus fully on how to "be holy both in body and in spirit". So use that singleness as an opportunity to really seek the Lord with all your heart, through extra prayer, Bible study, and memorization.

2) It opens up possibilities for ministry. I Corinthians 7:35
While there are ways in which a spouse can strengthen us in ministry, and Vi has certainly been that for me—being single enables you to "attend upon the Lord without distraction". From mission projects, to canvassing programs, to evangelism or health training schools—the opportunities for a single person are endless. But once you are married and start having kids, these all quickly start to become more difficult.

3) It enables you to practice self-control. I Corinthians 7:37
Some think that marriage means all our selfish desires will suddenly be fulfilled, and we'll no longer have to worry about them any more. The reality is quite different. True love requires us to consistently put the needs of our partner first, and failure to do that can make a marriage intolerable. Being single gives you a chance to cultivate the tools you need to you need to live a life of integrity. "He that standeth stedfast in his heart, having no necessity, but hath power over his own will" will discover that contributes directly to increased happiness in marriage.

You can probably think of other blessings that come with singleness. My advice, is to make the most of them. Those few years of singleness, God led me through were exactly what I needed. I spent endless hours internalizing the Word of God. I was able to engage in all sorts of ministry opportunities. And I learned countless lessons about how to deal with temptation, and walk in personal integrity. I wouldn't trade those years for anything.

And personally, I'm quite sure I would not have been near as ready for marriage without that time. If you are single right now: embrace it, and allow God to grow you through it.

One More Consideration

I should add one final reason Paul gives to persuade us to embrace the gift of singleness. And it's simply that times of persecution are just ahead. And having a wife, not to mention children, when Revelation's final scenes unfold, is going to make earth's final trial even more severe.

Paul urged singleness "for the present distress" (I Corinthians 7:26). And that not having a wife during difficult times would "spare" us much "trouble in the flesh" (I Corinthians 7:28). Having always lived in a peaceful country, I can't really imagine how hard it would be to see my spouse (or children) suffering in times of persecution. Can you?

But the freedoms we enjoy today will not last forever. Now, more than ever, "time is short" (I Corinthians 7:29). And when earth's final persecution does break out, it will be necessary that "they that have wives be as though they had none" (I Corinthians 7:30). And the closer we get to end, the more important staying single will become.

For the Ungifted

Paul certainly makes it clear that not all have the gift of singleness. And that there is nothing wrong with taking a husband or wife. And by implication, nothing wrong with looking for a partner. Nothing wrong with dating—at least not when done as outlined in the Bible.

But don't rush into this. Your first priority is to develop your own personal maturity, your character, your spirituality. Singleness is the perfect time to deepen your walk with Christ. To give Him time to heal your needy heart. Make the most of that time, to learn, and grow, and serve. You may never have the same level of freedom to pursue those things again.

And if you will focus on thriving, while single, and not compromise in any of your dating principles—God will do a work in your heart. He will change it from a needy heart, to a giving heart. And once you are ready to focus on serving another person unselfishly, God will bring that person into your life.

Tomorrow, we'll look at how to know when you have found the right partner.

The Gift of Singleness?
Worksheet

Explain why a time of singleness can be one of the biggest secrets to success in dating?

According to Paul, what are four benefits of singleness?

1.

2.

3.

4.

What should we do if we find ourselves single, but don't feel called to singleness?

Additional Notes:

Adam and Eve
Day 6

One of the most common questions young people ask when dating, is how to know if the person they are with presently is the one they are meant to marry. And unfortunately, our decision-making skills only get more and more problematic the more emotionally and physically connected we are. The stronger our feelings, the harder it gets to see things objectively!

Fortunately there are a number of things we can do to discern God's guidance on this. These first guidelines apply to pretty much any big decision—but are especially important in choosing a life partner.

Basic Decision-Making

First and foremost, every decision should be brought to the Word of God. If you are in a dating relationship, and contemplating marriage—you need to be spend more time than ever searching the Bible's pages for guidance. In a previous study, we saw that our partner needs to be a spiritually mature, and growing Christian, of our own denomination. If they don't meet this basic test, you have your answer already. But going beyond this, the Bible can give you insights into their character, your character, potential compatibility issues, and much more. Start looking for these insights, and try to remain open to them.

Assuming someone meets the basic biblical tests for a life partner, the next key to discerning God's will is prayer. If you are accustomed to praying once a day when single, I recommend praying three times a day when dating! Emotions can be tricky, and the heart is quite deceitful. But in prayer, we can ask God to help us see clearly, and to be more sensitive to His leading. If we are sincere in wanting to know His will about a person, God can help us notice hidden character flaws, or strengths, you might miss otherwise. And He can amplify any uneasiness we have about that person, or fill us with a deep abiding peace and calm. And perhaps most important of all, God can give us the courage and strength we need to break off a relationship that's not for our best good. Plead for guidance as if your whole future depends on it, because it might!

Third in line, is the importance of godly counsel. Seek out advice from those who know you well, and if possible, who know your partner. If possible, give these trusted advisors opportunities to get to know them, and observe them. Seek out people who have significant life experience, with successful marriages of their own. And who love you enough to tell you the truth. And most of all, people who are deeply spiritual, whose connection with God you respect. People are sometimes reluctant to share their real counsel, but if you are sincere about wanting to know their thoughts, and make an effort to draw it out—they will open up to you.

Among this list of counselors, be sure to include your parents. If you have godly parents who can guide you spiritually, you are especially fortunate. But even unbelieving parents often have good insights into our strengths and weaknesses and can see patterns we lack the experience to recognize. God promises special blessings to those who honor their parents—so give significant weight to the counsel of both sets of parents. And work hard to get the full support and encouragement from both sides of the family, before moving forward in this area.

Adam and Eve

Beyond these basic decision making principles, I believe we can glean additional insights into choosing a mate from the story of Adam and Eve. After all they are the archetypal couple, and theirs was the first marriage—the only wedding in fact, conducted by God Himself! Follow the pattern outlined there, and it may just help you to discern the right partner too.

Consider for example the following points:

1) Adam and Eve were both fully mature at creation. God is probably not going to make your life partner clear until you are ready to marry. And worrying about this question prematurely, is not helpful.

2) Adam was in a position to care for and provide for Eve. Achieving financial security is an important preparation for marriage. When this is lacking, it will put severe stresses and pressures on the relationship.

3) Adam was given a work to do before, before he was introduced to Eve. In fact, it was in naming the various animals that Adam first sensed his need for a companion. In the same way, you will be able to best discern the kind of life partner you need once your life work is clear.

4) Adam had to put his need for a spouse to sleep for a time, while God was busy getting Eve ready for him. You too may have to spend a period of time waiting alone, before God brings your spouse into your life.

5) Adam did not go searching for Eve. God brought her to him. In the same way, if you wait on God and trust Him to bring you a life partner, He will bring the right person at the right time. Go searching on your own, and you are liable to miss out on God's best plan. And finally,

6) Adam was absolutely awestruck by Eve's beauty when they met. In fact, all he could say was "whoa, man"! And the name stuck: woman. You can be sure God's choice for you will be captivatingly beautiful (or handsome), in your eyes, as well.

One Last Thought

At the beginning of this study, the question was raised—how can we know if the person we are with is the right one. The story of Adam and Eve suggests this question needs to be reversed. Because Adam followed the right order of things in God's plan for dating, he never had any question that she was the one God intended for him.

In other words, he waited to start dating until God had made clear who that right person was. Rather than dating to figure out if someone might be the right person, we should seek to discern that first, and only start dating then.

Dating someone we have no intention of marrying, just to pass the time, while we wait for someone better to come along—is wrong. It is unfair to the other person, and it may hurt us in the end as well. After all, if you end up finding yourself attached to the wrong person, when the right one finally does come along, you may just miss out on the true love of your life.

When God brought Eve to Adam, he knew she was the one. And if you trust God to bring your partner to you, you will too.

Adam and Eve
Worksheet

What makes it especially hard to be objective, and make wise decisions when choosing a life partner?

What are three basics of decision-making we need to apply to choosing a partner?

1.

2.

3.

Who especially should we consult with on this question? And why?

List 6 insights from the experience of Adam and Eve that can help us know how to choose the right mate?

1.

2.

3.

4.

5.

6.

Which should come first: dating, or discerning someone is God's choice for us? Why is it ideal to do things in this order?

Additional Notes:

Life With No Regrets
Day 7

Many years ago I heard a sermon on dating that began with an unusual verse—one of those verses you hear from the pulpit once in a lifetime—if that. But the speaker made a point that has stuck with me all the years since.

Here's the verse he used:

II Corinthians 7:2
Receive us; we have wronged no man, we have corrupted no man, we have defrauded no man.

In this passage, Paul was writing to the believers at Corinth, one of the ministry centers he had spent significant time at. In fact, according to Acts 18:11, he had spent there "a year and six months, teaching the word of God among them". During all that time, there wasn't one person that could point to anything Paul had done that was inappropriate. He hadn't wronged any one. He hadn't corrupted any one. He hadn't defrauded any one.

Not a single person, not a single time.

The speaker then made the profound point that this kind of life doesn't happen by accident. The only way to live a life like this, is to purpose ahead of time exactly how we will live. And then to follow through on that commitment. Or to put it differently, to live a life of no regrets—is to live a life of purpose.

Marriage with no Regrets

If there is one area of life you don't want bogged down with regrets, it's your marriage. Married life is tough enough in a sin-filled, selfish world. And the less baggage we bring into that relationship the better.

Through the years, Vi and I have had the privilege to work with many struggling couples—and more often than not, the problems they were experiencing, could be traced back to mistakes made years prior, often from before they were married. Those problems didn't surface right away, but they had a way of bubbling up eventually—until they were finally forced to deal with them. And that often proved to be a painful process.

The key to entering a marriage relationship without regrets is simple. You have to purpose ahead of time exactly how you will treat those you date, and then follow through on that commitment. A marriage without regrets is the direct result of dating with purpose.

Even if you have made mistakes in the past, you can choose from this day forward to commit yourself to God's plan. To aim for the highest level of moral purity. To focus on building strong spiritual friendships first. To wait on the Lord to reveal your life partner, before becoming emotionally attached. And to move toward marriage at the right time, and in the right way. Deliberately, intentionally, purposefully.

If you do those things, your wedding will not just be a nice ceremony—it will be a testament to the power of God to bring two people together, when they let Him lead. In fact, the whole ceremony will be filled with rich meaning.

The Wedding Ceremony

Vi and I didn't do everything perfectly when dating, but we tried hard to follow these principles I've been sharing closely. And our wedding was one of the happiest days of our life.

We designed our own wedding program, and included on it a long list of explanations for what the various symbols in our wedding meant to us. Consider some of the following, as examples:

1) Why do friends of the bride and groom sit on opposite sides of the church? In Bible times, marriage was a covenant between two families. Marriage is not just a temporary contract, but a lifelong covenant, where two families are joined together.

2) Why does the groom enter first? This signifies the man is initiating the covenant, and thus bears primary responsibility for fulfilling it. In the same way, God initiated covenants with many Bible characters, and assumed the greater responsibility for fulfilling them.

3) Why does the father walk the bride down the aisle? This action communicates that the bride's family fully endorses this union, and thus conveys the blessing of his family on the couple. And it reminded me of God bringing Eve to Adam.

4) Why does the bride wear a white dress? This not only symbolizes the purity of the bride, but even more, the purity with which the husband promises to treat his wife going forward. Just as Christ provides white raiment to the church, it made sense to us that the groom pay for the dress.

5) Why do the bride and groom make sacred vows to each other? These are special, lifelong promises to each other, formal commitments with unlimited liability, being made before God. These vows are at the heart of the marriage covenant.

6) What is the meaning of the bride's veil? Just as a veil separated the Most Holy Place from the rest of the temple, the bride's veil symbolizes that the physical relationship is not to be entered into, until after the vows have been completed.

7) Why does a minister perform the ceremony, and in a church? Marriage is more than just a civil union. It is a spiritual union establish by, and preserved by heaven. Just as God performed the first wedding, I believe He still seals hearts together.

8) Why do attendees sign a guest book? Each guest, in effect, is an official witness to the covenant established that day, and a reminder of the promises made. For this reason, we had our guests sign the guest book after the wedding rather than before.

9) Why is a special invitation given to the reception? The Bible talks about the marriage supper of the lamb in connection with the salvation we will enjoy, when Christ returns for His people. The wedding reception says the couple look forward to that day, and will remain true to Christ until then.

You can probably think of other symbols in the wedding ceremony that have important religious significance, and you may assign different meanings to some of these. But my point in sharing all this, is that because we were intentional about seeking God all through our dating relationship—we came to see our wedding as a highly spiritual event, a grand celebration, the birth of a supernatural union, ratified in heaven itself. We could enter our marriage with the full assurance of God's blessing on us.

We could enter marriage with no regrets.

I'm more convinced now than ever that the more closely we follow God's plan for dating, the more fully we will be able to enjoy God's plan for marriage!

Life With No Regrets
Worksheet

What is the only way to live a life without regrets?

What can we do to help ensure we enjoy a marriage with no regrets?

When two people fully allow God to bring them together, how does that change a wedding ceremony?

Give examples of symbols in the wedding ceremony with spiritual significance?

Is it possible today to enter marriage with no regrets? Why or why not?

Additional Notes:

FAST Missions
Cutting-Edge Tools and Training

Ready to become a Revival Agent? FAST Missions can help! Our comprehensive training curriculum will give you the skills you need to take in God's Word effectively, live it out practically, and pass it on to others consistently.

Eager to start memorizing God's Word? Our powerful keys will transform your ability to hide Scripture in your heart.

Want to explore the secrets of "real life" discipleship? Our next level training zooms in on critical keys to growth, like Bible study, prayer, time management, and more.

Want to become a worker in the cause of Christ? Our most advanced training is designed to give you the exact ministry skills you need to see revival spread.

For more information, please visit us at:
WWW.FASTMISSIONS.COM

Study Guides

Looking for life-changing study guides to use in your small group or Bible study class? These resources have been used by thousands around the world. You could be next!

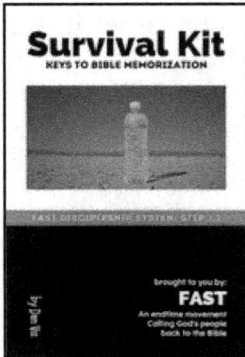

Survival Kit

Want to learn how to memorize Scripture effectively? These study guides will teach you 10 keys to memorization, all drawn straight from the Bible. Our most popular course ever!

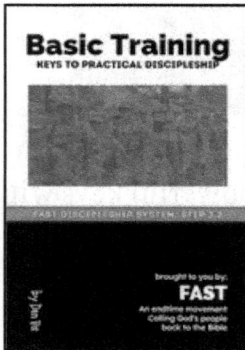

Basic Training

Discover nuts and bolts keys to the core skills of discipleship: prayer, Bible study, time management, and more. Then learn how to share these skills with others. It is the course that launched our ministry!

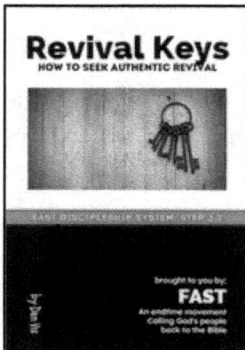

Revival Keys

Now as never before, God's people need revival. And these guides can show you how to spark revival in your family, church, and community. A great revival is coming. Are you ready?

Online Classes

Want to try out some of the resources available at FAST? Here is just a small sampling of courses from among dozens of personal and small group study resources:

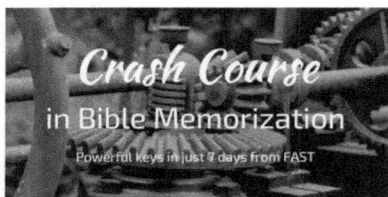

Crash Course
Discover Bible-based keys to effective memorization.
http://fast.st/cc

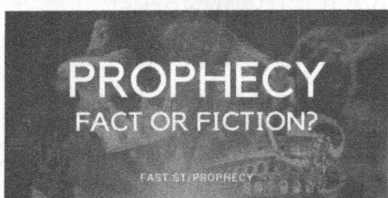

Fact or Fiction
Does the Bible really predict future events? You be the judge.
http://fast.st/prophecy

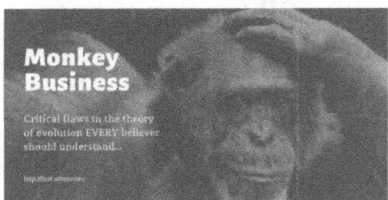

Monkey Business
Find out how evolution flunks the science test.
http://fast.st/monkey

Revive
Want more of God's Spirit? Learn how to pursue revival.
http://fast.st/revive

The Lost Art
Rediscover New Testament keys to making disciples.
http://fast.st/lostart

Digital Tools

FAST offers a number of powerful "apps for the soul" you can use to grow in your walk with God. And many of these are completely free to anyone with an account. Some of these include:

Review Engine
Our powerful review engine is designed to help ensure effective longterm Bible memorization. Give it a try, it works!

Bible Reading
An innovative Bible reading tool to help you read through the entire Bible, at your own pace, and in any order you want.

Prayer Journal
Use this tool to organize important requests, and we'll remind you to pray for them on the schedule you want.

Time Management
Learn how to be more productive, by keeping track of what you need to do and when. Just log in daily and get stuff done.

For more information about more than twenty tools like these, please visit us at *http://fast.st/tools*.

Books

If the content of this little book stirred your heart, look for these titles by the same author.

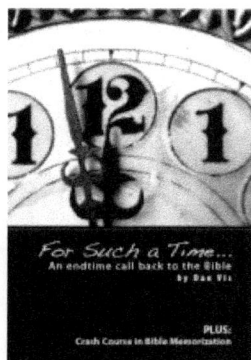

For Such A Time...
A challenging look at the importance of memorization for the last days, including topics such as the Three Angel's messages and the Latter Rain.

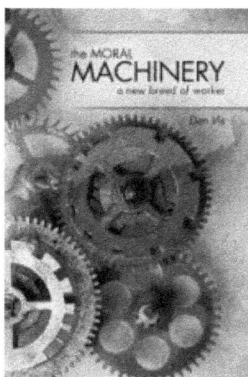

Moral Machinery
Discover how our spiritual, mental, and physical faculties work together using the sanctuary as a blueprint. Astonishing insights that could revolutionize your life!

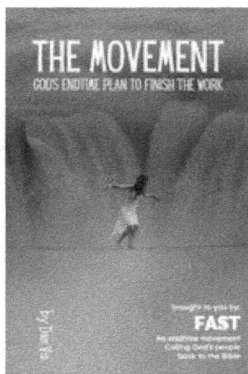

The Movement
Discover God's plan to finish the work through a powerful endtime movement. Gain critical insights into what lies just ahead for the remnant!